Cake
in a
Jar

A Recipe Collection

Jackie Gannaway

Published in Austin, TX by COOKBOOK CUPBOARD, P.O. Box 50053, Austin, TX 78763 (512) 477-7070

ISBN 0-885597-06-1

Artwork by Ann Moon   KCC Logo by Mosey 'N Me

Mail Order Information

To order a copy of this book send a check for $3.95 + $1.50 for shipping (TX residents add 8 % sales tax) to Cookbook Cupboard, P.O. Box 50053, Austin, TX 78763. Send a note asking for this title by name. If you would like a descriptive list of all the fun titles in The Kitchen Crafts Collection, send a note asking for an order blank. People who enjoy baking might enjoy one or all of the three books in the Friendship Breads series, "Friendship Breads, Starters and Recipes", "Fat Free Friendship Breads, Starters and Recipes" and "Fruit Friendship Breads, Starters and Recipes". You might also enjoy "Cake Mix Cakes" - over 50 recipes that begin with cake mixes. All the Kitchen Crafts titles are $3.95.

Introduction

Cakes and breads in jars make wonderful gifts. They are simple to make and fun to receive. This book has over 20 recipes for cakes and breads in jars. For a complete list of all recipes in this book, look in the Index on the last page.

A sample recipe for baking in a clay flowerpot is included as well as several ideas for baking in clay saucers.

The cake is stored in the same jar in which it is baked. The jars are sterilized as are the lids. When you put the hot sterilized seals on the hot jars a seal is formed. If sealed correctly they will last several months without refrigeration.

However, keeping cakes indefinitely is not the objective of this. It is just a fun, different way to give a food gift to a friend. It is recommended that cakes be kept in refrigerator for prolonged storage. They can also be frozen. Put an "expiration date" of two months or so on the ones you give away. People tend to think these are so cute that they look at them for a year or so and then forget when they received them.

These are ideal for mailing. Send one as a birthday cake. Attach a candle (one of those musical candles is fun) with a note to take the cake out of the jar, insert and light the candle and sing Happy Birthday for you!

Each recipe in this book makes 4 to 8 jar cakes, with most recipes making 6 jar cakes.

Other Recipes - Other Pans

Try some of your favorite baking recipes in jars. (Recipes for pound cakes or nut/fruit breads work best.) Reduce the temperature 25 degrees from what is called for in your recipe because glass bakes hotter than metal baking pans.

All of these recipes can also be baked in small clay flowerpots (4 1/2" diameter by 4" tall). These can be wrapped in colored cellophane and a few silk flowers tied on with raffia. They make good Easter or Springtime gifts, good gifts for gardeners and the garden club. Line the flowerpot with heavy duty foil. Grease the foil. Put 1 cup batter in the flowerpot and bake at 350 (not 325 as for the glass jars).

All of the recipes can also be baked in regular cake pans - use a Bundt or tube pan or 2 loaf pans for each recipe. When baking in regular pans, bake at 350 and for about the same time as called for when baking in jars. Test for doneness with a toothpick.

Other Size Jars

You can bake smaller, individual cakes in a jar by using wide-mouth half-pint jars. Use 1/2 cup batter in this size jar and bake about 30 minutes. Test for doneness.

You can bake in one and one-half pint jars (Ball brand is a good shape for this). You will have to experiment with this. I suggest baking one cake first to make sure you have the time and temperature right for this size or you could waste all your batter. After the first one works, then fill the remaining jars. Try 1 3/4 cup batter in this size jar and baking it an hour or longer at 300. Test with a long bamboo skewer for doneness. If it is not completely done, the batter will sink and form a hole in the middle of the cake.

Decorating Jars

To decorate jars for giving, cut a circle of gingham or calico with pinking shears and lay it on top of the seal. Then screw on the ring - the ring holds the cloth in place. You can tie a ribbon and bow around the ring.

Or cut a circle of wrapping paper and put over the lid. Hold in place with a rubber band and tie a ribbon around that.

For Easter, or a Springtime look, you can use a paper doily, or a Battenburg lace doily (available at fabric shops and crafts stores). Place over the lid, hold in place with a rubber band and tie with a ribbon. Insert a silk flower under the ribbon for added decoration.

If you make handmade Christmas ornaments, it is nice to attach one to the top of the jar, so you are giving both the ornament and the cake, and the ornament is part of the jar decoration.

Buy decorated labels to label the jars.

Recipe Cards

If you want to give the recipe with the cake, the copyright on this book is relaxed to allow a few copies for personal use. Take the book to a full service copy shop and ask them to copy it on colored card stock (heavier than paper). You will have a choice of colors. The colored ink in this book will show up black on the copy. Choose a color of card stock to match the season or occasion of the gift. Show the copyright sentence on the page opposite the Table of Contents to the copy shop so they will know they have copyright permission to copy it.

You may want to give a copy of the procedure on the next page along with the recipe. Copy it on the same colored card stock.

I hope you have as much fun with these as I did testing and experimenting with the recipes.

Jackie Gannaway

Cake in a Jar - Procedure

Use wide mouth pint size canning jars. You can buy them at larger grocery stores. They are sold individually and by the dozen. When you buy them they come with seals (the round flat thing that covers the jar opening) and rings (the band that screws on). You can use jars again. Sterilize them each time. You need new seals each time. They are sold separately.

Be sure there are no nicks or cracks in the glass. Wash the jars, seals and rings in hot, soapy water. Rinse and place jars and rings in large pot. Fill with water and boil 15 minutes, covered. (It is easier to place jars in pan on the stove and fill the pan there rather than filling at the sink and carrying it to the stove.) Place seals and rings in a small pan of boiling water and simmer until ready to use. Dry jars and grease very well, bottom and sides (don't spray). Put **ONLY 1 CUP BATTER** in each jar. More than that will rise over the top.

Place jars on a baking sheet (not touching each other) and bake for time indicated. Remove one jar at a time from oven (use both hands and two hot pads - jars are very hot). Put a hot seal on jar and screw on the ring. Don't screw the ring too tight.

The cake will slide right out of the jar with a strong shake or two when ready to serve. If it doesn't, run a flat bladed table knife around the cake and that will allow it to slide out. You can also shake the cake loose (don't unseal it) before you give it. That way it will be obvious as it slides inside the jar how they are to get it out.

Lemon Pound Cake in a Jar

2 2/3 cups sugar
2 sticks butter
4 eggs
1/3 cup fresh lemon juice
1 tsp. vanilla
1 tsp. lemon extract

2 Tb. grated lemon peel
3 1/2 cups flour
1 tsp. baking powder
2 tsp. baking soda
1 tsp. salt

1. In large bowl, cream sugar and butter with electric mixer.
2. Add eggs and mix well.
3. Add lemon juice and extracts and mix well.
4. Place dry ingredients in a separate large bowl and blend with a whisk.
5. Add creamed ingredients to dry ingredients and mix with whisk and spoon.
6. Place 1 cup batter each in 6 well greased one pint wide-mouthed canning jars. Wipe batter from rim.
7. Place jars on a baking sheet. Bake at 325 for 55 to 60 minutes or a toothpick inserted in center comes out clean.
8. Wipe rims. Place hot sterilized seals and rings on hot jars. Keep in refrigerator for prolonged storage.

Makes 6 jars.

Lemon Blueberry Bread in a Jar

2 2/3 cups sugar
2/3 cup shortening
4 eggs
2/3 cup water
1 Tb. fresh lemon juice
2 Tb. grated lemon zest
1 tsp. lemon extract

3 1/2 cups flour
1/2 tsp. cinnamon
1 tsp. baking powders
2 tsp. baking soda
1 tsp. salt
2 cups fresh or frozen
    blueberries
2/3 cup chopped nuts

1. In a large bowl, cream sugar and shortening with electric mixer.
2. Add eggs and mix well.
3. Add water, lemon juice, lemon zest and lemon extract.
4. Place all dry ingredients in a separate large bowl and blend with a whisk. Reserve 1/2 cup dry ingredients.
5. Add creamed ingredients to dry ingredients and mix with whisk and spoon.
6. If using frozen blueberries, rinse well. Place blueberries and pecans in medium bowl and toss with reserved 1/2 cup dry ingredients. Add to batter and stir by hand until blended.
7. Place 1 cup batter each in 6 sterilized well greased one pint wide-mouthed canning jars. Wipe batter from rim.
8. Place jars on a baking sheet. Bake at 325 for 45 to 55 minutes or a toothpick inserted in center comes out clean.
9. Wipe rims. Place hot sterilized seals and rings on hot jars. Keep in refrigerator for prolonged storage.

Makes 6 jars.

Peach Pound Cake in a Jar

2 2/3 cups sugar	1 tsp. baking powder
2 sticks butter	2 tsp. baking soda
4 eggs	1 tsp. salt
1 tsp. vanilla	2 cups peeled, chopped
2 tsp. almond extract	fresh peaches
3 1/2 cups flour	1/2 cup sour cream

1. In large bowl, cream sugar and butter with electric mixer.
2. Add eggs and mix well.
3. Add vanilla and almond extract and mix well.
4. Place dry ingredients in a separate large bowl and blend with a whisk.
5. Add creamed ingredients to dry ingredients and mix with whisk and spoon.
6. Gently stir in chopped peaches and sour cream.
7. Place 1 cup batter each in 7 well greased one pint wide-mouthed canning jars. Wipe batter from rim.
8. Place jars on a baking sheet. Bake at 325 for 50 minutes until a toothpick inserted in center comes out clean.
9. Wipe rims. Place hot sterilized seals and rings on hot jars. Keep in refrigerator for prolonged storage.

Makes 7 jars.

Rum Cake in a Jar

1 yellow cake mix
1 (4-serving) vanilla
  instant pudding
4 eggs

1 cup oil
1/2 cup water
3/4 cup rum

1. Place cake mix and pudding mix in a large bowl.
   Blend with a whisk.
2. Add eggs, oil, water and rum and mix with electric mixer
   for 2 minutes.
3. Place 1 scant cup batter each in 6 well greased one pint
   wide-mouthed canning jars. Wipe batter from rim.
4. Place jars on a baking sheet. Bake at 325 for 45 minutes
   until a toothpick inserted in center comes out clean.
5. Wipe rims. Place hot sterilized seals and rings on hot jars.
   Keep in refrigerator for prolonged storage.

Makes 6 jars.

Vanilla Pound Cake in a Jar

2 2/3 cups sugar
2 sticks butter
4 eggs
1/3 cup water
2 Tb. vanilla

3 1/2 cups flour
1 tsp. baking powder
2 tsp. baking soda
1 tsp. salt

1. In large bowl, cream sugar and butter with electric mixer.
2. Add eggs and mix well.
3. Add water and vanilla and mix well.
4. Place dry ingredients in a separate large bowl and blend with a whisk.
5. Add creamed ingredients to dry ingredients and mix with whisk and spoon.
6. Place 1 cup batter each in 6 well greased one pint wide-mouthed canning jars. Wipe batter from rim.
7. Place jars on a baking sheet. Bake at 325 for 55 to 60 minutes or a toothpick inserted in center comes out clean.
8. Wipe rims. Place hot sterilized seals and rings on hot jars. Keep in refrigerator for prolonged storage.

Makes 6 jars.

Chocolate Cake in a Jar

2 2/3 cups sugar
2/3 cup shortening
4 eggs
1/3 cup buttermilk
1/3 cup cold brewed coffee
1 Tb. vanilla
3 1/2 cups flour

2 tsp. cinnamon
1 tsp. baking powder
2 tsp. baking soda
1 tsp. salt
6 (1 oz.) squares unsweet-
     ened chocolate, melted
2/3 cup chopped nuts

1. In large bowl, cream sugar and shortening with electric mixer.
2. Add eggs and mix well.
3. Add buttermilk, coffee and vanilla and mix well.
4. Place dry ingredients in a separate large bowl and blend with a whisk.
5. Add creamed ingredients to dry ingredients and mix with whisk and spoon.
6. Blend in melted chocolate.
7. Place 1 cup batter each in 6 well greased one pint wide-mouthed canning jars. Wipe batter from rim.
8. Place jars on a baking sheet. Bake at 325 for 45 minutes or a toothpick inserted in center comes out clean.
9. Wipe rims. Place hot sterilized seals and rings on hot jars. Keep in refrigerator for prolonged storage.

Makes 6 jars.

Gingerbread in a Jar

2 cups brown sugar
2/3 cup sugar
2/3 cup shortening
4 eggs
1/2 cup molasses

3 1/2 cups flour
1 tsp. baking powder
2 tsp. baking soda
1 tsp. salt
1 tsp. ginger
1/2 tsp. cinnamon
1/4 tsp. cloves

1. In large bowl, cream sugars and shortening with electric mixer.
2. Add eggs and mix well.
3. Add molasses and mix well.
4. Place dry ingredients and spices in a separate large bowl and blend with a whisk.
5. Add creamed ingredients to dry ingredients and mix with whisk and spoon.
6. Place 1 cup batter each in 6 well greased one pint wide-mouthed canning jars. Wipe batter from rim.
7. Place jars on a baking sheet. Bake at 325 for 50 to 55 minutes or a toothpick inserted in center comes out clean.
8. Wipe rims. Place hot sterilized seals and rings on hot jars. Keep in refrigerator for prolonged storage.

Makes 6 jars.

Pumpkin Bread in a Jar

2 2/3 cups sugar
2/3 cup shortening
4 eggs
2/3 cup buttermilk
1 (16 oz.) can pumpkin

3 1/2 cups flour
1 tsp. baking powder
2 tsp. baking soda
1 tsp. salt
1 1/2 Tb. pumpkin pie spice
2/3 cup chopped nuts

1. In large bowl, cream sugar and shortening with electric mixer.
2. Add eggs and mix well.
3. Add buttermilk and mix well.
4. Add pumpkin and mix well.
5. Place dry ingredients in a separate large bowl and blend with a whisk.
6. Add creamed ingredients to dry ingredients and mix with whisk and spoon.
7. Stir in nuts.
8. Place 1 cup batter each in 7 well greased one pint wide-mouthed canning jars. Wipe batter from rim.
9. Place jars on a baking sheet. Bake at 325 for 55 minutes until a toothpick inserted in center comes out clean.
10. Wipe rims. Place hot sterilized seals and rings on hot jars. Keep in refrigerator for prolonged storage.

Makes 7 jars.

Cranberry Nut Bread in a Jar

1 cup sugar
1/2 stick butter
1 egg
1 cup buttermilk
1/4 cup cranberry juice cocktail
1/2 tsp. vanilla

3 cups flour
1 tsp. baking powder
1 tsp. baking soda
1/2 tsp. salt
1 1/4 cups chopped
    cranberries
1 1/2 cups chopped nuts

1. In large bowl, cream sugar and butter with electric mixer.
2. Add egg and mix well.
3. Add buttermilk, cranberry juice and vanilla and mix well.
4. Place dry ingredients in a separate large bowl and blend with a whisk. Reserve 1/2 cup dry ingredients.
5. Add creamed ingredients to dry ingredients and mix with whisk and spoon.
6. Place cranberries and nuts in medium bowl and toss with 1/2 cup reserved dry ingredients. Gently stir cranberries and nuts into batter.
7. Place 1 cup batter each in 4 well greased one pint wide-mouthed canning jars. Wipe batter from rim.
8. Place jars on a baking sheet. Bake at 325 for 45 minutes until a toothpick inserted in center comes out clean.
9. Wipe rims. Place hot sterilized seals and rings on hot jars. Keep in refrigerator for prolonged storage.

Makes 4 jars.

Cherry Nut Bread in a Jar

1 cup sugar
1/2 stick butter
1 egg
1 cup buttermilk
1/4 cup maraschino cherry juice
1/2 tsp. almond extract
3 cups flour

1 tsp. baking powder
1 tsp. baking soda
1/2 tsp. salt
1 tsp. nutmeg
1 1/4 cups chopped frozen
  dark sweet cherries,
  thawed and rinsed
1 1/2 cups chopped nuts

1. In large bowl, cream sugar and butter with electric mixer.
2. Add egg and mix well.
3. Add buttermilk, cherry juice and almond extract and mix well.
4. Place dry ingredients in a separate large bowl and blend with a whisk. Reserve 1/2 cup dry ingredients
5. Add creamed ingredients to dry ingredients and mix with whisk and spoon.
6. Place cherries and nuts in medium bowl and toss with reserved 1/2 cup dry ingredients. Gently stir chopped cherries and nuts into batter.
7. Place 1 cup batter each in 4 well greased one pint wide-mouthed canning jars. Wipe batter from rim.
8. Place jars on a baking sheet. Bake at 325 for 45 minutes until a toothpick inserted in center comes out clean.
9. Wipe rims. Place hot sterilized seals and rings on hot jars. Keep in refrigerator for prolonged storage.

Makes 4 jars.

Carrot Cake in a Jar

2 2/3 cups sugar
2/3 cup shortening
4 eggs
2/3 cup water
2 tsp. vanilla
3 1/2 cups flour
1 tsp. baking powder

2 tsp. baking soda
1 tsp. salt
2 tsp. cinnamon
2 cups peeled, grated
  carrots
2/3 cup chopped nuts

1. In large bowl, cream sugar and shortening with electric mixer.
2. Add eggs and mix well.
3. Add water and vanilla and mix well.
4. Place dry ingredients in a separate large bowl and blend with a whisk.
5. Add creamed ingredients to dry ingredients and mix with whisk and spoon.
6. Gently stir in grated carrots and nuts.
7. Place 1 cup batter each in 6 well greased one pint wide-mouthed canning jars. Wipe batter from rim.
8. Place jars on a baking sheet. Bake at 325 for 55 minutes until a toothpick inserted in center comes out clean.
9. Wipe rims. Place hot sterilized seals and rings on hot jars. Keep in refrigerator for prolonged storage.

Makes 6 jars.

Zucchini Bread in a Jar

2 cups sugar	1 tsp. baking powder
1 cup oil	1 tsp. baking soda
3 eggs	1/2 tsp. salt
2/3 cup water	1 1/2 Tb. cinnamon
1 tsp. vanilla	3 cups grated zucchini
3 1/4 cups flour	1 cup chopped nuts

1. In large bowl, cream sugar and oil with electric mixer.
2. Add eggs and mix well.
3. Add water and vanilla and mix well.
4. Place dry ingredients in a separate large bowl and blend with a whisk.
5. Add creamed ingredients to dry ingredients and mix with whisk and spoon.
6. Stir in grated zucchini and nuts.
7. Place 1 cup batter each in 6 well greased one pint wide-mouthed canning jars. Wipe batter from rim.
8. Place jars on a baking sheet. Bake at 325 for 55 to 60 minutes or a toothpick inserted in center comes out clean.
9. Wipe rims. Place hot sterilized seals and rings on hot jars. Keep in refrigerator for prolonged storage.

Makes 6 jars.

Banana Nut Bread in a Jar

2 2/3 cups sugar
2/3 cup shortening
4 eggs
2/3 cup buttermilk
1 tsp. vanilla
3 1/2 cups flour
1/2 tsp. ginger

2 tsp. baking soda
1 tsp. baking powder
1 tsp. salt
2 cups mashed ripe
   bananas
2/3 cup chopped nuts

1. In large bowl, cream sugar and shortening with electric mixer.
2. Add eggs and mix well.
3. Add buttermilk and vanilla and mix well.
4. Place dry ingredients in a separate large bowl and blend with a whisk.
5. Add creamed ingredients to dry ingredients and mix with whisk and spoon.
6. Gently stir in mashed bananas and nuts.
7. Place 1 cup batter each in 7 well greased one pint wide-mouthed canning jars. Wipe batter from rim.
8. Place jars on a baking sheet. Bake at 325 for 45 minutes until a toothpick inserted in center comes out clean.
9. Wipe rims. Place hot sterilized seals and rings on hot jars. Keep in refrigerator for prolonged storage.

Makes 7 jars.

Fresh Apple Nut Cake in a Jar

2 2/3 cups sugar
2/3 cup shortening
4 eggs
2/3 cup buttermilk
3 1/2 cups flour
1 tsp. baking powder

2 tsp. baking soda
1 tsp. salt
2 tsp. cinnamon
2 cups peeled, grated
  apples
2/3 cup chopped nuts

1. In large bowl, cream sugar and shortening with electric mixer.
2. Add eggs and mix well.
3. Add buttermilk and mix well.
4. Place dry ingredients in a separate large bowl and blend with a whisk.
5. Add creamed ingredients to dry ingredients and mix with whisk and spoon.
6. Gently stir in chopped apples and nuts.
7. Place 1 cup batter each in 7 well greased one pint wide-mouthed canning jars. Wipe batter from rim.
8. Place jars on a baking sheet. Bake at 325 for 50 minutes until a toothpick inserted in center comes out clean.
9. Wipe rims. Place hot sterilized seals and rings on hot jars. Keep in refrigerator for prolonged storage.

Makes 7 jars.

Italian Cream Cake in a Jar

2 2/3 cups sugar	3 1/2 cups flour
1 stick butter	1 tsp. baking powder
4 eggs	2 tsp. baking soda
2/3 cup buttermilk	1 tsp. salt
1 Tb. vanilla	2 cups flaked coconut
	2/3 cup chopped nuts

1. In large bowl, cream sugar and butter with electric mixer.
2. Add eggs and mix well.
3. Add buttermilk and vanilla and mix well.
4. Place dry ingredients in a separate large bowl and blend with a whisk.
5. Add creamed ingredients to dry ingredients and mix with whisk and spoon.
6. Add coconut and nuts and blend.
7. Place 1 cup batter each in 6 sterilized well greased one pint wide-mouthed canning jars. Wipe batter from rim.
8. Place jars on a baking sheet. Bake at 325 for 55 to 60 minutes or a toothpick inserted in center comes out clean.
9. Wipe rims. Place hot sterilized seals and rings on hot jars. Keep in refrigerator for prolonged storage.

Makes 6 jars.

Pina Colada Cake in a Jar

2 2/3 cups sugar
1 stick butter
4 eggs
2/3 cup drained pineapple juice
1 Tb. coconut extract
3 1/2 cups flour

1 tsp. baking powder
2 tsp. baking soda
1 tsp. salt
1 (20 oz.) can crushed pineapple, well drained
1 cup flaked coconut

1. In large bowl, cream sugar and butter with electric mixer.
2. Add eggs and mix well.
3. Add pineapple juice and coconut extract and mix well.
4. Place dry ingredients in a separate large bowl and blend
   with a whisk.
5. Add creamed ingredients to dry ingredients and mix with
   whisk and spoon.
6. Gently stir in pineapple and coconut.
7. Place 1 scant cup batter each in 8 well greased one pint
   wide-mouthed canning jars. Wipe batter from rim.
8. Place jars on a baking sheet. Bake at 325 for 45 minutes
   until a toothpick inserted in center comes out clean.
9. Wipe rims. Place hot sterilized seals and rings on hot jars.
   Keep in refrigerator for prolonged storage.

Makes 8 jars.

Apricot Nut Bread in a Jar

1 cup sugar
1 stick butter
3 eggs
2/3 cup orange juice
2 tsp. orange extract
3 1/2 cups flour

3 tsp. baking powder
1/2 tsp. baking soda
1/2 tsp. salt
1 (6 oz.) bag dried apricots, chopped
1 cup chopped nuts

1. In large bowl, cream sugar and butter with electric mixer.
2. Add eggs and mix well.
3. Add orange juice and extract and mix well.
4. Place dry ingredients in a separate large bowl and blend with a whisk. Reserve 1/2 cup dry ingredients.
5. Add creamed ingredients to dry ingredients and mix with whisk and spoon.
6. Place apricots and nuts in a medium bowl and toss with reserved 1/2 cup dry ingredients. Gently stir apricots and nuts into batter.
7. Place 1 scant cup batter each in 6 sterilized well greased one pint wide-mouthed canning jars. Wipe batter from rim.
8. Place jars on a baking sheet. Bake at 325 for 55 minutes until a toothpick inserted in center comes out clean.
9. Wipe rims. Place hot sterilized seals and rings on hot jars. Keep in refrigerator for prolonged storage.

Makes 6 jars.

Apple Butter Bread in a Jar

2 1/4 cups packed brown sugar
1 stick butter
4 eggs
1 cup apple butter
3 1/2 cups flour

1 tsp. baking powder
2 tsp. baking soda
1 tsp. salt
1 1/2 Tb. pumpkin pie spice
1 cup golden raisins
2/3 cup chopped nuts

1. In large bowl, cream brown sugar and butter with electric mixer.
2. Add eggs and mix well.
3. Add apple butter and mix well.
4. Place dry ingredients in a separate large bowl and blend with a whisk. Reserve 1/2 cup dry ingredients.
5. Add creamed ingredients to dry ingredients and mix with whisk and spoon.
6. Place raisins and nuts in a medium bowl and toss with 1/2 cup reserved dry ingredients. Gently stir raisins and nuts into batter.
7. Place 1 cup batter each in 6 sterilized well greased one pint wide-mouthed canning jars. Wipe batter from rim.
8. Place jars on a baking sheet. Bake at 325 for 50 minutes until a toothpick inserted in center comes out clean.
9. Wipe rims. Place hot sterilized seals and rings on hot jars. Keep in refrigerator for prolonged storage.

Makes 6 jars.

Caramel Nut Cake in a Jar

2 cups brown sugar	3 1/2 cups flour
2/3 cup sugar	1 tsp. baking powder
2 sticks butter	2 tsp. baking soda
4 eggs	1 tsp. salt
2/3 cup milk	1 cup chopped nuts
1 Tb. vanilla	

1. In large bowl, cream sugars and butter with electric mixer.
2. Add eggs and mix well.
3. Add milk and vanilla and mix well.
4. Place dry ingredients in a separate large bowl and blend with a whisk.
5. Add creamed ingredients to dry ingredients and mix with whisk and spoon.
6. Gently stir in nuts.
7. Place 1 cup batter each in 6 well greased one pint wide-mouthed canning jars. Wipe batter from rim.
8. Place jars on a baking sheet. Bake at 325 for 50 minutes until a toothpick inserted in center comes out clean.
9. Wipe rims. Place hot sterilized seals and rings on hot jars. Keep in refrigerator for prolonged storage.

Makes 6 jars.

Irish Soda Bread in a Jar

2/3 cups sugar
2 Tb. butter, melted
1 egg
1 1/2 cups buttermilk
3 cups flour

1 Tb. baking powder
1 tsp. baking soda
1 tsp. salt
1 1/2 cups raisins
1 Tb. caraway seeds (opt.)

1. In large bowl, mix sugar, melted butter, egg and buttermilk with electric mixer.
2. Place dry ingredients in a separate large bowl and blend with a whisk.
3. Add wet ingredients to dry ingredients and mix with whisk and spoon.
4. Gently stir in raisins and optional caraway seeds.
5. Place 1 scant cup batter each in 5 well greased one pint wide-mouthed canning jars. Wipe batter from rim.
6. Place jars on a baking sheet. Bake at 325 for 45 minutes until a toothpick inserted in center comes out clean.
7. Wipe rims. Place hot sterilized seals and rings on hot jars. Keep in refrigerator for prolonged storage.

Makes 5 jars.

Kahlua Cake in a Jar

1 yellow cake mix	1 cup oil
1 (4-serving) chocolate	1/2 cup water
instant pudding	3/4 cup Kahlua
4 eggs	

1. Place cake mix and pudding mix in a large bowl. Blend with a whisk.
2. Add eggs, oil, water and Kahlua and mix with electric mixer for 2 minutes.
3. Place 1 scant cup batter each in 6 well greased one pint wide-mouthed canning jars. Wipe batter from rim.
4. Place jars on a baking sheet. Bake at 325 for 45 minutes until a toothpick inserted in center comes out clean.
5. Wipe rims. Place hot sterilized seals and rings on hot jars. Keep in refrigerator for prolonged storage.

Makes 6 jars.

Amaretto Cake in a Jar

1 white cake mix
1 (4-serving) vanilla
    instant pudding
4 eggs

1 cup oil
1/2 cup water
3/4 cup Amaretto

1. Place cake mix and pudding mix in a large bowl. Blend with a whisk.
2. Add eggs, oil, water and Amaretto and mix with electric mixer for 2 minutes.
3. Place 1 scant cup batter each in 6 well greased one pint wide-mouthed canning jars. Wipe batter from rim.
4. Place jars on a baking sheet. Bake at 325 for 45 minutes until a toothpick inserted in center comes out clean.
5. Wipe rims. Place hot sterilized seals and rings on hot jars. Keep in refrigerator for prolonged storage.

Makes 6 jars.

Fabulous Brownie Pudding Cake

1 brownie mix	eggs
water	vanilla ice cream

1. Mix brownie mix with water and eggs as called for on the package for chewy brownies.
2. Line clay saucers (4 1/2" diameter) with heavy duty foil. Grease foil.
3. Spread 2/3 cup brownie batter in each saucer.
4. Bake at 350 for 30 minutes. (They won't be done in the middle.)
5. Serve immediately topped with a scoop of vanilla ice cream.

A regular size brownie mix will make 4 of these.

Put then in the oven when you sit down to dinner.
30 minutes later they will be ready just in time for dessert.

Baked Brownie Alaska with Strawberries

1 brownie mix	vanilla ice cream
water	4 egg whites
eggs	12 fresh strawberries

1. Mix brownie mix with water and eggs as called for on the package for chewy brownies.
2. Line clay saucers (4 1/2" diameter) with heavy duty foil. Grease foil.
3. Spread 1/3 cup brownie batter in each saucer.
4. Bake at 350 for 25 minutes.
5. Make serving size balls of ice cream. Place ice cream balls in a flat dish and freeze hard.
6. Cool brownies completely.
7. In a small bowl, beat egg whites and sugar with electric mixer until stiff peaks form.
8. Hull and slice 2 strawberries per serving.
9. Place frozen ice cream ball on each brownie. Cover with strawberry slices.
10. Cover entire surface with meringue, being careful to seal all openings. Mound meringue high.
11. Heat at 450 for 3 to 5 minutes, watching closely.
12. Serve immediately.

A regular size brownie mix will make 5 to 6 of these. It you use a family size brownie mix use 6 egg whites for meringue.

You can have the brownies baked and cooled in the saucers and the ice cream balls frozen. Let your children or guests assemble these while you beat the egg whites.

Individual Pies

1 (21 oz.) can cherry pie filling	1 box refrigerated pie crusts

1. Line 4 (4 1/2") clay saucers with heavy duty foil. Grease foil.
2. Unfold the two prepared pie crusts. Cut circles of crust big enough to line the saucers. (I have a mixing bowl that cuts just the right size circle.) Place crusts into saucers and press gently into place. Prick crust with a fork.
3. Roll the crust scraps and cut 1/2" wide strips.
4. Divide the cherry pie filling among the four saucers.
5. Use the strips of pie crust to make lattice tops.
6. Bake 45 minutes at 350 or until lightly browned.

Follow this procedure to make any pie recipe in saucers.